LEGENDARY HEROES
OF THE WILD WEST

BILL PICKETT
AFRICAN-AMERICAN RODEO STAR

William R. Sanford &
Carl R. Green

Enslow Publishers, Inc.

40 Industrial Road   PO Box 38
Box 398   Aldershot
Berkeley Heights, NJ 07922   Hants GU12 6BP
USA   UK

http://www.enslow.com

Library of Congress Cataloging-in-Publication Data

Sanford, William R. (William Reynolds), 1927–
    Bill Pickett : African-American rodeo star / William R. Sanford and
Carl R. Green.
        p. cm.—(Legendary heroes of the Wild West)
    Includes bibliographical references and index.
    Summary: Describes the life and accomplishments of the son of a former slave
whose unusual bulldogging style made him a rodeo star.
    ISBN 0-89490-676-3
    1. Pickett, Bill, ca. 1860–1932—Juvenile literature. 2. Afro-American
cowboys—Biography—Juvenile literature. [1. Pickett, Bill, ca. 1860–1932.
2.Cowboys. 3. Afro-Americans—Biography.] I. Green, Carl R. II. Title.
III. Series: Sanford, William R. (William Reynolds), 1927– Legendary
heroes of the Wild West.
GV1833.6.P5S25   1997
636.2'0092—dc20
[B]
                                                                    96-1891
                                                                    CIP
                                                                    AC

Printed in the United States of America

10 9 8 7 6 5 4

Illustration Credits: William R. Sanford and Carl R. Green, pp. 39, 40;
Taylor (Texas) Public Library Archives, p. 11; Texas Department of Highways,
pp. 6, 12; Western History Collection, University of Oklahoma, pp. 8, 15, 18,
20, 23, 26, 27, 31, 34, 35.

Cover Illustration: Paul Daly

CONTENTS

AUTHORS' NOTE

A rodeo is a live-action show that displays the riding and roping skills of cowboys. The first rodeos were held in Mexico. By 1888 they had spread to the United States. Modern rodeo competitions include eight events: bareback bronc riding, saddle bronc riding, bull riding, calf roping, steer roping, team roping, barrel racing, and bulldogging. No one knows who introduced the first seven events. That is not the case with bulldogging. Credit for inventing this dramatic way of throwing a full-grown steer belongs to an African-American cowboy named Bill Pickett. Today, Pickett is recognized as one of the Wild West's legendary cowboys. This is his true story.

1

A COWBOY STEALS
THE SHOW

$\sim\!\cdot\!\sim\!\cdot\!\sim\!\cdot\!\sim\!\bullet\!\bullet\!\sim\!\cdot\!\sim\!\cdot\!\sim\!\cdot\!\sim$

By 1905 big crowds were turning out to watch rodeo cowboys do their stuff. At the Fort Worth Fat Stock Show that year, Bill Pickett thrilled fans with his bulldogging. One of the spectators was rancher Zack Miller. Zack and his brothers were planning a big Western show at their 101 Ranch. He wasted no time in signing Bill for his show.

Bill had seen big ranches in his native Texas. None matched the 101, which lay in north-central Oklahoma's Cherokee Strip. Thousands of cattle grazed on the 110,000 acres of sweet grass. Bill did not know it, but he had found a home.

On June 11, 1905, thousands of rodeo fans gathered in nearby Guthrie. They made their way to the ranch by buggy, wagon, and on foot. Well-dressed men and women drank soda water and talked about the upcoming show.

Bulldogger Bill Pickett starred in the 1905 Fort Worth Fat Stock Show. It was here that Zack Miller hired Pickett to perform his acrobatic bulldogging for the 101 Ranch Wild West Show in Oklahoma.

Around noon, rain clouds formed to the northeast. Zack's brother, Joe, watched the sky darken and shook his head. If the storm hit, he would have to refund the ticket money.

A Ponca medicine man named Sits-on-a-Hill stepped forward. "Big blow. Big rain. No show," he told Joe. For five steers, he added, he would stop the rain. Joe told Sits-on-a-Hill he had a deal. The medicine man danced and sang and pounded on a drum. As the clouds reached the nearby river he screamed and shook a shell at the sky. Moments later, as if by magic, the storm veered to the east.[1]

The sun came out. A band played as Zack Miller and his brothers Joe and George led the grand parade. Behind them came two hundred Native American horsemen. The aging Apache warrior Geronimo rode with them. Bill Pickett rode with the cowboys and cowgirls who brought up the rear. Among them was cowhand Tom Mix. Mix later starred in dozens of silent films.

The show kicked off with a buffalo hunt. Geronimo shot his buffalo from the back seat of a car. Ranch cooks later served barbecued hump meat to the show's special guests. Next came the trick riding and roping. Then it was Bill's turn.

The announcer cried, "The next event will be Bill Pickett, the Dusky Demon from Texas. [Bill] will leap from the back of a running horse onto a running steer. [He will] throw the steer with his bare hands and teeth."[2] A gate swung open and a half-ton steer dashed out of his pen. Behind him streaked a cowboy known as a hazer. It was his job to keep the steer running in a straight line.

All eyes turned to the star bulldogger. In 1905 Bill was in his mid-thirties. He stood five feet, seven inches, and weighed 145 pounds. He had a slim waist, big hands, and powerful shoulders. His eyes and skin were dark. Strong white teeth gleamed under a small mustache. On this day he was dressed like a Mexican bullfighter.

Bill urged his horse forward. Spradley quickly drew up beside the fast-moving steer. Timing his jump nicely, Bill launched himself onto the steer's back. Grabbing a horn in each hand, he dropped to the side and dug his heels into the ground. At the same time, he twisted the steer's neck upward. As the head came up, Bill sank his teeth into the tender upper lip. An instant later he let go of the horns, flung his hands wide, and dove backward. The steer followed him down. It lay quietly on its side as the crowd cheered. Bill's bite-'em style had stopped the show.[3]

The applause brought a broad smile to Bill's weathered face. A day later Sits-on-a-Hill shared a secret that made Bill laugh. The medicine man had known when he started his dance that most storms turned east at the river.

During his lifetime, Bill Pickett toppled more than five thousand head of cattle with his celebrated bite-'em style. Some of the steers he threw weighed up to half a ton. Under modern rules, a bulldogger is not allowed to bite the animal's lip.

2

A BULLDOGGER
GROWS UP IN TEXAS

Bill Pickett's grandmother moved to Texas in the 1850s. Unlike the state's white settlers, she did not come of her own free will. Welborn and Alexander Barton brought her with them as one of their fifty-two slaves. In 1854, while the Barton wagon train was moving through Louisiana, Grandma Pickett gave birth to Bill's father. She named him Thomas Jefferson Pickett and called him Tom.

The Bartons settled in central Texas near Austin. The end of the Civil War in 1865 gave Tom Pickett and the other slaves their freedom. In 1870 sixteen-year-old Tom married Mary Gilbert. Both Tom and Mary were of mixed African-American, Native American, and Anglo descent. Mary soon gave birth to a son named Willie M. Family tradition dates the birth as December 5, 1870. Census records suggest a date in 1871. As often happens, the boy was known by more than one name. His family called him Willie. As he grew up, his friends and fans knew him as Bill.[1]

Tom moved his growing family to the outskirts of Austin. There he raised vegetables on a few rented acres. The produce found a market in the nearby city. Tom also worked at odd jobs. The hard labor did not bring in much money. In those days an African American was lucky to make fifty cents a day.

Bill was the oldest of thirteen Pickett children. What he lacked in height he made up in strength and agility. He also had a quick mind and a keen sense of humor. The one-room school he attended did not challenge him. He learned to read and write, but dropped out after the fifth grade. That was common among poor children, white and black. Their parents needed them to work in the fields. Many country schools kept their doors open only four or five months a year.

When it came to horses and cattle, Bill was a fast learner. Each year, thousands of longhorn cattle moved through Austin on their way to stockyards in Kansas. Bill learned to read cattle brands and to throw a lasso. He also proved that he had a way with horses. The risk of being kicked, bitten, or thrown by a half-wild mustang did not worry him.

As a student of cattle, young Bill knew that longhorns sometimes hid in thick brush. Even if a cowboy reached them, the brush kept him from throwing his lasso. When

As a young cowboy, Bill Pickett lived across the street from his uncle's house on East Second Street in Taylor, Texas. Bill was living in Taylor when he joined two of his brothers in a business called the Pickett Brothers Broncho Busters and Rough Riders.

he was ten, Bill saw a local rancher use dogs to recover the strays. The dogs weighed fifty to sixty pounds and were part bulldog. They were trained to grab and hold a cow's upper lip in their teeth. Subdued by the pain, the longhorn would stand quietly until a cowboy arrived with a rope. In honor of the dogs' breed, the technique was called bull-dogging.

Bill thought about what he had seen. He weighed more than a bulldog. Why couldn't he use the same method? The next time he came upon a lone calf, he grabbed it by the ears. As its head came up, he sank his teeth into its upper lip. Then he let go of the ears and flipped backward. To his delight, the calf flopped over on its side.

On his way to school one day, Bill saw some cowboys

branding calves. Some of the larger calves were giving them trouble. Bill told the cowboys he could hold any calf—with his teeth. They laughed at what sounded like a silly boast, but agreed to let him try. After a cowboy roped and threw a calf, it was Bill's turn. He sank his teeth into the calf's upper lip, then signaled the cowboys to get on with the branding. To their surprise, the calf lay quietly as they applied the red-hot iron. When Bill released his hold, the calf shook its head and trotted off.[2]

The cowboys spread the word. Young Bill Pickett, they said, could "bulldog" a calf. No one guessed that the bite-'em technique would make him famous.

Modern rodeos feature many of the same events that thrilled audiences a century ago. Bulldogging, however, is the only event whose invention is credited to a single cowboy—the immortal Bill Pickett.

3

FROM WORKING COWBOY TO RODEO STAR

By the time he was fifteen, young Bill Pickett was a working cowboy. Chasing longhorns through the thick brush gave him plenty of chances to practice his bite-'em technique. Unable to swing a lasso, he would catch a steer by the horns. Then he would twist its head up and clamp his teeth on its lip. A moment later the steer would be lying on the ground.

Ranchers paid Bill five dollars for a work week of eighty hours or more. With a week's wages, Bill could buy a good razor and a .32-calibre pistol—and have nearly three dollars left over. For fun and extra spending money, he entered Sunday bronc-riding contests. Before long he was riding the meanest horses around. After applauding the bone-jarring rides, onlookers dropped coins into his hat.

In the late 1880s the Picketts moved to Taylor, Texas.

The small town lay thirty miles northeast of Austin. It was in Taylor that Bill fell in love with Maggie Turner. He married her in December 1890. In the years that followed, Maggie gave birth to nine children. Seven girls survived, but the couple's two sons died as infants.

Bill served as deacon in a Baptist church. He held Sunday school classes and services in his home. His faith was sorely tested during the year he went blind. No one knows the cause. The blindness may have been the result of a head injury or an infection. Eleven months later, Bill's sight returned as suddenly as it had vanished.[1] The family felt its prayers had been answered.

The 1890s were busy years. Bill and his brothers went into business as the Pickett Brothers Broncho Busters and Rough Riders. In their ads they promised to "ride and break all wild horses with much care. . . . Catching and taming wild cattle a specialty."[2] For two weeks each summer, Bill trained with the National Guard. He was a private when the Spanish-American War broke out in 1898. His unit volunteered to go to Cuba. The army took a cavalry outfit instead.

In 1900 rancher Lee Moore booked Bill into rodeos across Texas, Arizona, and Colorado. Bill enjoyed the travel and the applause. He did not like the fact that Moore kept the lion's share of the ticket money. In 1903 promoter Dave McClure gave Bill a better deal. On posters, McClure called him the Dusky Demon. The nickname was vital. McClure could not bill his star as an African

Tom Mix was a fellow cowboy and good friend of Bill Pickett. Both men performed in the 101 Ranch Wild West Show. Mix went on to star as the hero of many Hollywood westerns.

American. If he had done so, racial prejudice would have kept white cowboys from competing against him.[3]

Western newspapers reported Bill's feats in glowing terms. In 1904 John Dicks Howe of *Harper's Weekly* came west to see for himself. He was awed. Howe wrote, "Twenty thousand people watched . . . a mere man . . . attack a fiery, wild-eyed, and powerful steer and throw it by his teeth."[4] When Bill fell backward with the steer's upper lip in his teeth, the animal fell on top of him. The crowd held its breath until the steer rolled over. Bill stood up, smiling and unhurt.

Zack Miller said that one of Bill's most dramatic exploits took place in 1905. Other accounts place the event in 1914. Either way, the site was New York City's Madison Square Garden. Will Rogers, an expert roper who later became a famous humorist, was Bill's hazer that night. A steer burst from the chute, raced across the arena, and jumped the barrier. People screamed and scattered. The steer scrambled up the steps that led to the balcony.

Bill spurred his horse and chased the steer up the steps. Rogers rode close behind, shaking out his lasso. The cowboys caught the runaway at the third balcony. Bill jumped and caught the horns just as Rogers lassoed the steer's hind legs. The bulldogger held the head steady as Rogers backed his horse down the stairs. Step by step, they pulled the steer back to the arena.

News of Bill's heroics spread like wildfire. The Wild West Show played to sellout crowds for the rest of its stay.

4

ON TOUR WITH THE 101 RANCH SHOW

Bill's fame was spreading. Dave McClure booked him for fairs and rodeos across the West and into Canada and Mexico. Bill performed in San Francisco soon after the great earthquake of 1906. The sight of the shattered city stayed with him the rest of his life. Although Bill refused to bulldog buffalo, he did take on an elk in El Paso, Texas. Bill toppled the long-legged beast without biting its upper lip. He did not want to risk being sliced up by the elk's huge antlers.

In 1907 the Miller brothers signed Bill to tour with their show. The 101 Ranch Wild West Show opened in Chicago. Then it moved on to the Jamestown Exposition in Virginia. Bill paid a price for the cheers he earned there. The steer he was bulldogging rolled over on him. The injuries kept him in bed for a week. That was all the inaction he could take. He was shaky and sore, but he climbed back on Spradley for the next day's show.[1]

Of all Bill's horses, Spradley was his favorite. The first time Bill saw him, the stallion had been near death. Bill cut out a splinter and cleaned out the infection. Then he stayed with Spradley while the wound healed. When the bay coat gleamed with health again, Bill began the horse's training. Spradley was a fast learner. Onlookers swore that the horse knew what to do without being told.[2]

Bill went back to his home in Taylor when the tour ended. Maggie nursed his bruises and tried to talk him into retiring. Bill would not listen. In the spring of 1908, he jumped at the Millers' offer of a full-time job. During the season, Bill would tour with the Wild West Show. For the

rest of the year, he would work on the ranch. Bill signed a contract that paid him eight dollars a week plus room and board.

Bill moved his family to the 101 Ranch. For a time, the Picketts lived in two

Bill Pickett and his horse Spradley drew big crowds wherever the 101 Ranch Wild West Show spread its tent. Even though Bill risked his life each time he bulldogged a steer, the Millers paid their star only eight dollars a week.

large tents. They cooked and ate in one and slept in the other. The ranch did not have a school for the girls, however. Bill solved the problem by renting a house in Ponca City, nine miles away. At that time only six African-American families lived there. Their children were not allowed to go to school with whites. The school board set up a classroom for them in a church.

The show traveled through the Midwest in 1908. During one stretch it rained for fifty straight days. Bill and Spradley slipped and skidded as they splashed after hard-running steers. Bill went back to the ranch when the long season ended in December.

The Millers took the rest of the show to Mexico City. At 7,400 feet above sea level, the air was as thin as the gate receipts. No one had warned the Millers that Mexicans preferred bullfights to rodeos. Soon the show was losing a thousand dollars a day.

To make matters worse, Joe Miller had legal problems. When an advertised performer did not appear, the show was fined fifty pesos a day. The 101 Ranch posters promised Bill Pickett, but Bill was back in Oklahoma. Joe sent for his star bulldogger. Bill did not want to go to Mexico, but loyalty won out. He joined the show a few days later.

Manolo Bienvenida and other top bullfighters watched Bill perform. Afterward, they bragged that they could bulldog, too—only faster. The local papers said that biting a steer's lip was disgusting. Bill Pickett, the stories added, lacked a bullfighter's grace and courage.

Joe found Bienvenida in a café. He said he admired the bullfighter's skill, but doubted that he could bulldog a steer, Pickett style. Do it, Joe added, and I'll give a thousand pesos to charity. Bienvenida accepted the challenge.[3]

The time for the test came and went. Bienvenida did not show up. At last he sent word that his contract kept him from taking foolish risks. In front of reporters, Joe accused the bullfighter of being a coward. The affair was building toward a showdown.

Weeks before the 101 Ranch Wild West Show appeared in a town, advance men pasted posters on the local barns. Touring with the show kept Bill away from his family for months at a time.

5

SHOWDOWN
IN THE BULLRING

~•~•~•~•~•~◆~◆~•~•~•~•~•~

Joe Miller offered to match Bill Pickett against a fighting
bull. To sweeten the pot, he put up a purse of five thousand
pesos. The bet called for Bill to stay in the ring for fifteen
minutes. For five of those minutes, he had to be in direct
contact with the bull. Miller stood to win five thousand
pesos plus all the gate receipts. If Bill lost, the bullring
would pay his funeral costs.

Bullfight fans lined up to buy tickets. They wanted to
see the American die in the bullring. Only then did Miller
tell Bill about the bet. Bill shrugged and said he could
throw any bull in Mexico.[1] Bienvenida and his friends
chose a bull named Bonito for Bill to fight. The black bull
had survived an earlier bullfight. His life had been spared
because he fought bravely and well.

On December 23, 1908, over 25,000 fans packed the

bullring. Porfirio Díaz, the president of Mexico, took his seat to a blare of trumpets. The bullfighters carried a black coffin as they circled the ring. Bill knew the coffin was meant for him. At the last minute the district governor tried to cancel the fight. In his ruling, he named Bonito as the bull Bill must not fight. The bullring manager, unwilling to cancel the event, found a loophole in the order. Instead of Bonito, he matched Bill against a ferocious bull named Little Bean.

It was late in the afternoon when Bill rode in on Spradley. He wore a Stetson hat, a red shirt, jeans, and boots. A team of four cowboys followed, ready to serve as hazers. A trumpet sounded, and Little Bean dashed into the ring.

Spradley spun away as Little Bean charged. The hazers tried to drive the bull in a straight line, but he was too quick. Bill closed in and tried in vain to grab the horns. His failure told him that getting closer to the bull would risk Spradley's life. As the crowd jeered, he left the ring to ask for a change of horses. Miller was afraid the crowd would riot. He told Bill to finish the job, "or we're all gonna get killed."[2]

Little Bean charged again. This time Bill would not let Spradley sidestep. Blood spurted as needle-sharp horns gored Spradley's hindquarters. Bill slid down, faced the angry bull, and locked his hands on the bloody horns. Little Bean shook his head, tossing Bill from side to side. Then the bull pawed at the stubborn bulldogger and tried to gore him. As a last resort he smashed him against the wall. Through it all Bill kept his grip on the slippery horns.

The bloodthirsty fans threw bottles, bricks, and boards. A well-aimed beer bottle broke three of Bill's ribs and opened a nasty gash. Blood trickled into his boots. Gasping for breath in the thin air, Bill lost his grip. He dropped to the ground in front of Little Bean. Bill had hung on for over seven minutes. He had won the bet, but he was in danger of losing his life.

Little Bean tried to gore the helpless bulldogger. For once his deadly horns missed their target. Before the bull could charge again, a cowboy drew him off by waving a red shirt. Bill scrambled to safety as the crowd screamed its rage. More bottles and bricks rained down. The cowboys took refuge behind an iron gate.

As Bill checked Spradley's wounds, an old man stepped forward. He said he was an expert in treating horn

Rodeo crowds usually cheered when Bill Pickett rode into the ring. In Mexico City, angry bullfight fans booed him for what they thought was an insult to their sport. They showered Bill with bottles and seat cushions during his life-or-death struggle with a fighting bull.

wounds. He peeled two red bananas and thrust the pulp deep into the wounds. Ten minutes later Spradley was back on his feet. Thanks to the strange treatment, the wounds healed quickly.

President Díaz dispatched his troops to escort the Americans to their hotel. A doctor cleaned and dressed Bill's wounds. Later, Bill explained why he had not bull-dogged Little Bean. Fighting bulls, he pointed out, have short, thick necks. "If I had gotten the kind of hold I usually get, . . ." he said, "I would have stayed with that bull until he starved to death."[3]

6

RIDING THE
SHOW TRAIN

~~~~~~~~~~~~~~~~~~~~

Bill's broken ribs healed slowly. When he could ride again, he helped work the 101 Ranch's cattle. The show took to the road again in the spring of 1910. This time the Millers had to leave their star behind. Bill was not in shape to start bulldogging again.

Maggie tried to talk Bill into staying home with his family. Her nagging led to heated quarrels. Bill's daughters did not share their mother's fear that he was risking his life. The girls loved to hear him talk about his bulldogging feats. Maggie's heart softened, too, when she saw him mourn the death of his sons. If the boys had lived, he would have trained them to be cowboys, too.[1]

The Miller Brothers' 101 Ranch Real Wild West Show was growing. The cast and work crews now traveled in six sleeper cars. Horses, mules, steers, oxen, and buffalo filled

MILLER BROS
101 RANCH

REAL WILD WEST

JOSEPH C. MILLER

MILLER BROS.
&
EDW. ARLINGTON
EQUAL OWNERS

GEORGE
L. MILLER

ZACK
T. MILLER

Joseph, Zack, and George Miller owned the sprawling 101 Ranch near Guthrie, Oklahoma. In addition to raising cattle, they organized a popular Wild West show. Adding Bill Pickett helped insure the show's success.

seven livestock cars. Nine flatcars carried the tents and equipment. At each stop the workers put up the huge show tent. It covered an area equal to two football fields.

By September 1910 two of Bill's replacements had been injured. Once more the Millers sent for Bill. He told Maggie good-bye and returned to the show. Despite his starring role, he did not expect star treatment. He bunked in one of the sleeper cars and ate in the cook tent. If a cowboy could not perform, Bill often filled in for him.

Each show opened with a grand parade. Bill rode atop a wagon that carried two buffalo, Nip and Mary. Nip may have served as the model for the old buffalo nickel. The action started with trick riding and roping. Teams of riders then staged a Pony Express ride and a stagecoach robbery. Native Americans danced and chanted to the rhythmic beat of drums. A Roman rider vaulted over four horses and landed on the back of a fifth.

Bill's bulldogging was the show's high point. The

Millers billed him as "the greatest sweat and dirt cowboy that ever lived—bar none."[2] People came prepared to cheer, and Bill gave them their money's worth. After his bite-'em act the steer ropers took over. Next came square dancing on horseback and women sharpshooters. Cowboys caught a horse thief, raced a team of Russian Cossacks, and rode bucking broncos. Bill sometimes delighted the crowd by mounting one of the broncos. The show ended with a wagon train massacre staged by Cheyenne warriors. Afterward, the audience sang "Home Sweet Home."

In January 1910 Bill leased some land from the 101 Ranch. Because the land was close to the ranch, he could spend more time at home. Maggie took charge of the

The 101 Ranch Wild West Show attracted enthusiastic crowds in small towns across America. The performers traveled from their train to the show grounds in a grand parade. Wherever he appeared, Bill Pickett drew some of the loudest cheers.

house, the garden, a cow, and a few pigs. Instead of herding cattle, Bill managed the ranch's buffalo herd. The Millers used some of the buffalo in the show. They sold the excess as breeding stock.

The next three years slipped by quickly. Despite Maggie's pleas, Bill refused to give up his show tours. By 1912 his salary had risen to $12 a week. He put on his risky act in twenty-two states and three Canadian provinces that year. Two near-disasters marred the tour. On the way to Milwaukee, a fire burned some parade wagons. Later, a train wreck smashed the calliope and killed five horses. Bill escaped injury in both mishaps.

Back at the ranch, Bill spent the winter breaking horses. By the spring of 1913, he was on the road again. The new show was bigger than ever. Bill kept his top billing, even though he no longer threw steers by biting their lips. The humane society had won its battle to outlaw the bite-'em technique.[3]

Bill thrilled crowds almost daily until the show closed in October. Then he boarded a train for New York. It was time to take his act overseas.

7
BULLDOGGING IN FOREIGN LANDS

Showman Edward Arlington picked Bill to join an all-star show bound for Argentina. The group sailed on November 1, 1913. Riding bucking broncos had not prepared Bill for the ship's rolling motion. His stomach rebelled. He was seasick for most of his twenty-five days at sea.

In Buenos Aires, Arlington slipped his cast through customs. He could not do the same with the livestock. One of the horses had a disease called glanders. To keep the disease from spreading, inspectors put all of the show's horses to death. Arlington bought Argentine horses to replace them. Bill thanked his lucky stars that Spradley was safe at home.[1]

It was December. Buenos Aires was warmed by the southern hemisphere's summer sun. Bill thrilled the large crowds by bulldogging "green" Argentine steers. These steers had never been thrown before. They ran, kicked, and dodged to escape him. Bill took them down with his old bite-'em style. In a land where the rancher was king, no one charged him with cruelty.

The fans loved it when Bill dressed like an Argentine cowboy. The applause inspired him to show off all his tricks. Once he had his teeth clamped on a steer's lip, he sometimes took the critter down without using his hands. On other days he faked an injury and bulldogged with one arm in a sling. When asked why he did not use a rope, Bill gave his stock answer. "Ropes is all right for hanging people," he said. "But they gets in the way when ya' wants to rope a steer."[2]

Bill knew enough Spanish to talk to the Argentineans he met. No one insulted him because he was black. He ate roast beef in sidewalk cafés and smoked fine cigars. A wealthy rancher asked him to visit his spread, but Arlington refused to let him go. A second offer was easier to turn down. Bill said no to a chance to bulldog an alligator.[3]

A telegram brought Bill back to New York. Zack Miller was taking a show to England. Bill played New York for two weeks, then packed for the trip. The performers pitched their tents in London on April 29, 1914.

Zack scheduled a show for King George V and Queen Mary. The royal couple and their guests broke two rules that day. First, they stayed to see the entire show. According to custom, they should have left early. Second, King

The 101 Ranch Wild West Show was much more than a rodeo. The Miller brothers recreated moments from western history, including stage coach robberies and Pony Express mail deliveries.

George actually clapped for one of the bronc riders. Queen Mary saw the unkingly act and slapped his hands. Zack's daughter Virginia saw the slap. "I didn't think," she told her father, "that anybody could slap a king!"[4]

Bill did not use his bite-'em style in England. Even so, English animal lovers were upset by his act. Twisting a steer's neck, they said, was "horrible steer torture." The police arrested Bill and fined him $25. Zack paid the fine—and arranged to have Bill fined each week. The publicity was worth every cent.

The Earl of Lonsdale took Bill to visit his country home. The green English countryside reminded Bill of the

Texas hill country. At last the earl's yellow Mercedes stopped in front of Lowther Castle. It was the biggest house Bill had ever seen. He said the dining hall alone was half as big as the 101 Ranch's barn.

After an eight-course banquet, the men met in the smoking room. Bill held center stage with stories of his bulldogging exploits. One man wondered how someone Bill's size could throw a steer barehanded. Bill had heard the question before. "I can lift a two-hundred-pound bag of salt over my head with one movement," he said. "People tell me that's pretty strong."[5]

Zack was planning a tour of Europe, just as Buffalo Bill had done in 1889. His plans fell apart when World War I broke out. On August 7, the British army seized the show's horses and wagons. Zack collected $80,000 for his property, but the show had to close. There was nothing to do but sail for home.

8

A SHOWBIZ CAREER WINDS DOWN

⁓⁓⁓⁓⁓⁓⁓⁓⁓⁓⁓⁓

Bill returned to the 101 Ranch in time to appear in a silent film. By 1915 he was back on the road with the 101 Ranch show. The Millers, however, believed that the United States would soon be drawn into World War I. They sold out at the end of the 1916 season.

The United States entered the war in 1917. Bill was forty-seven, too old to join the army. He returned to the ranch as a working cowboy. Bulldogging was still in his blood, however. At a Sand Springs, Oklahoma, rodeo in 1920, he missed his steer and landed face first. When he stood up his face was a mass of scrapes and cuts. Bill took time out for first aid and then asked for a second chance. With only his eyes showing through the bandages, he quickly bulldogged his steer. The crowd paid tribute to his grit by showering him with coins.

Bill Pickett called the 101 Ranch his home for much of his adult life. Too old for army duty during World War I, he spent the war years working as a ranch hand. The Miller brothers ran the spread from the headquarters building shown here.

Later that year, Bill showed up at a rodeo in Dewey, Oklahoma. He won the first day's bulldogging with a time of 24.2 seconds. He lost his steer on the second day, but won again on the third day. Minutes later Bill saw a wild longhorn kill one of his friends.[1] It was a grim reminder of the risks he took.

Wherever Bill went, he was billed as the inventor of rodeo bulldogging. Looking back, he guessed that he had bulldogged at least five thousand steers. Those steers sometimes weighed as much as a thousand pounds. In a modern rodeo some steers weigh as little as four-hundred pounds. Bill's best time was eight seconds. The modern record is 2.2 seconds.

After the Dewey Roundup, Bill moved his family to Oklahoma City. He found work at the stockyards and as a mill hand. The change pleased Maggie, who liked his regular hours. Bill endured the crowded city for three years, but ranch life was in his blood. In 1924, he returned to the 101. Bronc rider Florence Reynolds met him there. "He was a good, kind person," she said. "Everybody on the ranch liked Bill."[2]

A favorite ranch story featured Bill and a brown bear named Tony. Tony lived at the ranch zoo, where guests liked to watch him guzzle soda pop. On this day Tony was scheduled to appear in a movie that was being shot on the ranch. Bill sat in the cab of a flatbed truck, ready to drive the bear to the site. Tony, for reasons of his own, refused to climb into the truck. When treats and threats failed, a ranch hand lassoed the bear. A hard tug on the rope put Tony in motion. The bear scrambled into the truck bed, slid forward, and tumbled into the front seat. Bill grinned and

Hollywood film crews used the 101 Ranch as a setting for a number of silent films. Bill Pickett appeared in several movies, but never became a big star. He did earn top billing in a film called The Bull-Dogger.

put the truck in gear. With Tony wedged in beside him, he drove off to find the movie crew.[3]

Bill nearly lost more than his smile on a day in 1928. With his horse moving at a gallop, he tried to lasso a coyote. At that instant the horse stepped in a gopher hole and flipped end over end. Bill hit the ground first. The horse landed on top of him, its neck broken. Bill struggled to pull free, but he was pinned down. "I was afraid the horse would kick me, as my head was not very far from his heels," Bill said later.[4] After a long, anxious hour, his shouts brought help. A team of railroad workers pulled him free of the dead horse.

Some of the joy went out of Bill's life when Maggie died in 1929. By then his daughters had married and moved away. Alone and lonely, he lived in a small house on the ranch. Sad times had come to the Millers, too. Back in 1925 they had organized a new show that was half-rodeo, half-circus. It featured wild animal acts as well as bucking broncos. In 1931 heavy losses forced Zack Miller to close the show.

The closing hit Bill hard. The Millers were rich, weren't they? Where had all the money gone?

9

"THERE'LL NEVER BE ANOTHER BILL"

The 101 Ranch's problems were beyond fixing. The country was sinking into the Great Depression. Zack, the last of the Miller brothers, lost control of the ranch. In March 1932 the new owners were selling off some of the horses. Bill went to the corral to separate Zack's personal horses from the sales herd.

Bill was riding Hornet on that fateful day. His much-loved Spradley had died of old age. The first horse Bill lassoed was a wild three-year-old chestnut. As he pulled the horse toward him, another horse ran against the rope. Bill lost his grip, and the rope went slack. The chestnut chose that moment to lunge backward. The rope went taut, and the whiplash knocked Bill off his horse. As he lay sprawled in the dirt, the frightened chestnut kicked him in the head. Bill staggered to his feet, blood dripping from his mouth and nose. Then he fainted.[1]

A visitor drove Bill to the hospital in Ponca City. Bill spent fourteen days in a coma before he died on April 2, 1932. Two hundred friends and admirers showed up for the funeral. Zack buried his old friend on a hill that overlooked the ranch. Four years later, the Cherokee Strip Cowpunchers Association honored its only African-American member. The members chipped in to buy a sandstone marker for the grave. The carved letters say, BILL PICKETT, C.S.C.A.

Will Rogers used his radio program to say good-bye to his friend. "Bill Pickett never had an enemy," Rogers told his listeners. "Even the steers wouldn't hurt old Bill."[2] His warm feelings were not shared by everyone. Bill was sometimes barred from rodeos because he was African American. The 101 Ranch Show also ran into racial problems. In some towns, the police would not let the show open if Bill was on the cast list.

That prejudice may explain a glaring injustice. Almost forty years passed before Bill's fellow rodeo cowboys voted him into the National Rodeo Cowboy Hall of Fame at the Western Heritage Center in Oklahoma City. In 1971 he became the Hall of Fame's twentieth member and the first African American.

More honors followed. In 1987 the North Fort Worth Historical Society unveiled a statue of Bill. The heroic ten-foot bronze shows Bill throwing a thousand-pound longhorn. It stands on the lawn of the Cowtown Coliseum. In 1994 the U.S. Postal Service included Bill in its Legends of the West postage stamp set. Bill shared the honor with such Western immortals as Buffalo Bill, Wyatt Earp, and Sacagawea. No sooner had the stamps been issued than the Postal Service recalled them. The picture on the stamp, Bill's great-grandson pointed out, was that of Bill's brother Ben. A new printing in December fixed the error.[3]

Bill's hometown of Taylor, Texas, does its best to keep his memory alive. A memorial plaque stands in the park across from City Hall. The high school library displays

In 1994, Bill Pickett was honored by the United States Postal Series. His stamp appeared in a panel of twenty Legends of the West, alongside Buffalo Bill Cody, Kit Carson, and other heroes. The stamps had to be reprinted when the Postal Service learned that Bill's portrait was actually that of his brother Ben.

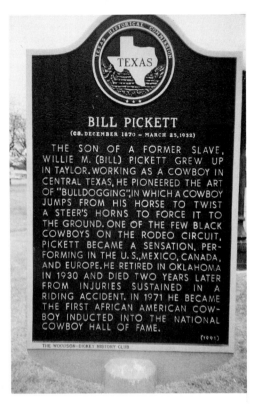

BILL PICKETT

(ca. DECEMBER 1870 – MARCH 25,1932)

THE SON OF A FORMER SLAVE, WILLIE M. (BILL) PICKETT GREW UP IN TAYLOR. WORKING AS A COWBOY IN CENTRAL TEXAS, HE PIONEERED THE ART OF "BULLDOGGING", IN WHICH A COWBOY JUMPS FROM HIS HORSE TO TWIST A STEER'S HORNS TO FORCE IT TO THE GROUND. ONE OF THE FEW BLACK COWBOYS ON THE RODEO CIRCUIT, PICKETT BECAME A SENSATION, PERFORMING IN THE U.S., MEXICO, CANADA, AND EUROPE. HE RETIRED IN OKLAHOMA IN 1930 AND DIED TWO YEARS LATER FROM INJURIES SUSTAINED IN A RIDING ACCIDENT. IN 1971 HE BECAME THE FIRST AFRICAN AMERICAN COWBOY INDUCTED INTO THE NATIONAL COWBOY HALL OF FAME.

(1991)

THE WOODSON–DICKEY HISTORY CLUB

On the main square in Taylor, a Texas historical marker tells the story of Bill's rise to national celebrity. In honoring Bill Pickett, the state also recognizes the contributions other African-American cowboys made to the history of the West.

photos, paintings, and books that tell Bill's story. In June 1992 Taylor held its first annual Bill Pickett Parade and Trail Ride. The ride led to nearby Noack. Legend says it was there that Bill first used his bite-'em technique.

Zack Miller was ahead of the pack. On the day Bill died, he sat down and wrote a poem called "Old Bill Is Dead." Near the end of his tribute, he says,

Like many men in the old-time West,
On any job, he did his best.
He left a blank that's hard to fill
For there'll never be another Bill.[4]

Bill Pickett would have felt mighty proud to be remembered so fondly.

CHAPTER NOTES

Chapter 1

1. Cecil Johnson, *Guts: Legendary Black Rodeo Cowboy Bill Pickett* (Fort Worth, Tex.: Summit Group, 1994), pp. 34–35.

2. Colonel Bailey C. Hanes, *Bill Pickett, Bulldogger: The Biography of a Black Cowboy* (Norman, Okla.: University of Oklahoma Press, 1977), p. 59.

3. Ibid., pp. 59–60.

Chapter 2

1. Colonel Bailey C. Hanes, *Bill Pickett, Bulldogger: The Biography of a Black Cowboy* (Norman, Okla.: University of Oklahoma Press, 1977), pp. 20–21.

2. Ibid., pp. 26–27.

Chapter 3

1. Cecil Johnson, *Guts: Legendary Black Rodeo Cowboy Bill Pickett* (Fort Worth, Tex.: Summit Group, 1994), pp. 56–57.

2. Colonel Bailey C. Hanes, *Bill Pickett, Bulldogger: The Biography of a Black Cowboy* (Norman, Okla.: University of Oklahoma Press, 1977), p. 36.

3. William Katz, *The Black West* (Seattle: Open Hand Publishers, 1987), p. 161.

4. Philip Durham and Everett L. Jones, *The Adventures of the Negro Cowboys* (New York: Bantam Books, 1969), pp. 97–98.

Chapter 4

1. Colonel Bailey C. Hanes, *Bill Pickett, Bulldogger: The Biography of a Black Cowboy* (Norman, Okla.: University of

Oklahoma Press, 1977), p. 69.

2. Robert H. Miller, *Reflections of a Black Cowboy* (Englewood Cliffs, N.J.: Silver Burdett Press, 1991), pp. 73–74.

3. Fred Gipson, *Fabulous Empire: Colonel Zack Miller's Story* (Boston: Houghton Mifflin Company, 1946), pp. 264–265.

Chapter 5

1. Fred Gipson, *Fabulous Empire: Colonel Zack Miller's Story* (Boston: Houghton Mifflin Company, 1946), p. 266.

2. Cecil Johnson, *Guts: Legendary Black Rodeo Cowboy Bill Pickett* (Fort Worth, Tex.: Summit Group, 1994), p. 83.

3. Colonel Bailey C. Hanes, *Bill Pickett, Bulldogger: The Biography of a Black Cowboy* (Norman, Okla.: University of Oklahoma Press, 1977), p. 104.

Chapter 6

1. Colonel Bailey C. Hanes, *Bill Pickett, Bulldogger: The Biography of a Black Cowboy* (Norman, Okla.: University of Oklahoma Press, 1977), p. 114.

2. William Katz, *The Black West* (Seattle: Open Hand Publishers, 1987), p. 160.

3. Fred Gipson, *Fabulous Empire; Colonel Zack Miller's Story* (Boston: Houghton Mifflin Company, 1946), p. 338.

Chapter 7

1. Cecil Johnson, *Guts: Legendary Black Rodeo Cowboy Bill Pickett* (Fort Worth, Tex.: Summit Group, 1994), pp. 105–106.

2. Colonel Bailey C. Hanes, *Bill Pickett, Bulldogger: The Biography of a Black Cowboy* (Norman, Okla.: University of Oklahoma Press, 1977), p. 41.

3. Ibid., p. 107.

4. Fred Gipson, *Fabulous Empire: Colonel Zack Miller's Story* (Boston: Houghton Mifflin Company, 1946), p. 341.

5. Johnson, p. 115.

Chapter 8

1. Colonel Bailey C. Hanes, *Bill Pickett, Bulldogger: The Biography of a Black Cowboy* (Norman, Okla.: University of Oklahoma Press, 1977), pp. 151–153.

2. Ibid., p. 158.

3. Cecil Johnson, *Guts: Legendary Black Rodeo Cowboy Bill Pickett* (Fort Worth, Tex.: Summit Group, 1994), pp. 143–144.

4. Hanes, p. 167.

Chapter 9

1. Colonel Bailey C. Hanes, *Bill Pickett, Bulldogger: The Biography of a Black Cowboy* (Norman, Okla.: University of Oklahoma Press, 1977), pp. 173–174.

2. Ibid., p. 180.

3. Cecil Johnson, *Guts: Legendary Black Rodeo Cowboy Bill Pickett* (Fort Worth, Tex.: Summit Group, 1994), pp. 171–172.

4. Ibid., pp. xvii–xviii.

GLOSSARY

branding—Burning the owner's mark into an animal's hide.

breaking—Training an untamed horse to obey its rider's commands.

broncos—Horses that have not been broken for riding. When a rider tries to mount a bronco the horse does its best to buck the rider off.

bulldogging—Throwing cattle to the ground so they can be branded. The term also describes a modern rodeo event.

calliope—An organlike instrument fitted with steam whistles and played from a keyboard.

chestnut—A reddish-brown horse.

chute—A passageway through which animals enter the arena at rodeos.

Civil War—The war between the North and the South, 1861–1865.

corral—A fenced area used to keep horses and cattle from straying.

customs—An agency authorized to inspect goods, baggage, and livestock that are being brought into a country.

deacon—A member of a Protestant church who has been selected to assist the minister.

gate receipts—Money taken in from the sale of tickets to a performance or sporting event.

glanders—A contagious, often fatal disease of horses and other equine species. The disease is marked by swollen lymph nodes, a nasal discharge, and skin and throat ulcers.

goring—A wound inflicted by an animal's horns.

Great Depression—The severe economic crisis of the 1930s. The period was marked by high unemployment and business failures.

grit—Western slang word for courage or bravery.

hazer—A rodeo rider who keeps steers running in a straight line so they can be bulldogged.

headliner—The top attraction at a show, rodeo, or sporting event.

humane society—An organization that tries to protect animals from cruel treatment.

lasso—A long rope with a running noose at one end. Cowboys use lassos to catch horses and cattle.

longhorn cattle—A breed of cattle with exceptionally long horns that once roamed wild on the Texas plains.

medicine man—A Native American who practices magic or sorcery for purposes of healing, divination, and control over natural events.

mustang—A wild horse of the North American plains.

peso—The basic unit of currency in Mexico. In Bill Pickett's day, a peso was roughly equal to an American dollar.

Pony Express—An overland mail service that used relays of riders and horses to carry the mail.

rodeo—An organized exhibition of cowboy skills.

Roman rider—Someone who performs acrobatics on horseback.

MORE GOOD READING ABOUT
BILL PICKETT

Durham, Philip, and Everett L. Jones. *The Adventures of the Negro Cowboys*. New York: Bantam Books, 1969.

Gipson, Fred. *The Fabulous Empire: Colonel Zack Miller's Story*. Boston: Houghton Mifflin Company, 1946.

Hanes, Colonel Bailey C. *Bill Pickett, Bulldogger: The Biography of a Black Cowboy*. Norman, Okla.: University of Oklahoma Press, 1977.

Johnson, Cecil. *Guts: Legendary Black Rodeo Cowboy Bill Pickett*. Fort Worth, Tex.: Summit Group, 1994.

Katz, William. *Black People Who Made the Old West*. New York: Thomas Crowell, 1977.

Miller, Robert H. *Reflections of a Black Cowboy*. Englewood Cliffs, N.J.: Silver Burdett Press, 1991.

O'Brien, Esse. *The First Bulldogger*. San Antonio, Tex.: Naylor Company, 1961.

INDEX